How to Analyze People

Learn how to understand and speed reading people by knowing body language signals and psychological techniques to become an expert on influencing and persuading everyone

Table of Contents

Introduction

Congratulations on downloading this book *How to Analyze People* and thank you for doing so. Get to understand how to analyze and know people from their behaviors and traits, learn skills to make you psychologically perceptive, understand communication vectors, and know more on behavioral traits and different personalities. This book is a guide aimed at achieving life skills that will make you adaptable in every way and enlighten you on people's differences and the qualities that make them. It primarily points out how you can live a life free from relationship problems or trouble getting along with people. It will help you establish a cohesive relationship with those around you as well as understand them. Enjoy your time going through it and get educated as well.

The following chapters will delve more on how to analyze people as well as the inner depths of the theories and ideologies behind them. They also point out possible solutions and tips on how to decode people and point out their traits and qualities that make them who they are or act the way they do. Lead a smooth communicative and interesting life as well as have enjoyable moments at it. The aim of this book being written is to educate, empower, and motivate you to get out of that comfort zone and push your limits in a quest to learn something new that affects you and the society around you. This information does not hold the final word on known theories but is one that can be relied on and followed. The book helps the typical person to the busiest of individuals on how to live life correlatively with knowledge and a sense of understanding and in a well cut out manner. Through extensive research and comparison from reliable and credible sources, this book therefore provides relevant information in the topics.

As you read through, take notes, steal ideas or two, try new techniques, and be informed on the key things and principles that could affect or help you in one way or another. To the reader, welcome to the new world as you open up your mental chambers for more knowledge!

Chapter 1: Analyzing People

How to Analyze People

You could be asking yourself on what this could be. Well analysis, analyzing people, more like an FBI or CIA kind of a thing? It may look like one complex activity but to your surprise, anyone can conduct it. You do not really have to have mind-reading powers or be a psychic to see through people. Analyzing people tends to be for a greater course, which is obviously to properly understand and to enhance smooth correlation among people. Whenever you find something intriguing or overwhelming, you tend to pay more attention to it and rather decode its peculiarity. Same case when you meet or encounter someone with a unique or rather unheard personality, curiosity takes the better part of you and you end up paying more attention to them. Putting them in the radar will both help you familiarize with their habitual characters and how to relate to them or behave yourself around them.

For you to be able to analyze someone, you need patience and a keen eye or ear or even both. Decoding someone will not be easy as you may get mixed signals, confusing new traits, or just a mix of sophistication in nature. Analyzing someone involves all your senses as a self-proclaimed investigator, as you will have to be keen on all pointers given or clues while conversing with them, or even their actions and reactions during specific situations. This will help you be able to know how to communicate with someone and carry yourself around them. As you will find, not everyone comes out as warm and welcoming to strangers, whereas others are open and easy going. Practicing this art equips you to have the ability to carve out the perfect formula or blueprint on how to handle different personalities.

For you to possess mastery in this discipline, you need to carry out a few activities. They include:

Build up a baseline (mental)

This is where you become the head of the observatory department. You tend to look out for behavioral traits during certain situations. How they act when nervous, do they stammer? Do they scratch their heads? Do they fold their hands? Do they blink repeatedly when cornered or under pressure? All this enables you to bring out and zero in on specific personality traits. Mannerisms often reflect what the true person is. Most of the time, people masquerade to be something they are not, but when confronted with a real issue that requires firm and concrete character, the so-called "wall" comes crumbling down revealing the true vulnerable self. You necessarily do not have to push someone to the wall to milk out their real traits. Behaviors always depict the true nature of someone and how their brains work, so keep an eye on that!

Comparison and Contrasting

Your so-called subject, are they acting the same way around everyone or do you have a two face situation at hand. Everyone obviously acts differently towards different people, not anyone gets that warm ear to ear smile, that tight bear hug, or even direct eye contact. So take note on how someone reacts around several people and jot down your findings. Of course, this is not a thing to conduct alone. If it is all the same outcomes, then you have a specific personality at hand, but if you get mixed reactions, or rather end up in a complex web of confusion, then worry not, just a little patience and pretty soon, your nut will soon crack!

Identify Personality Clues

As you have already encountered different people and gotten to adapt to them, you can point out their characters as per how they talk, walk, or even relate with others. Search for relatable pointers or unique qualities that blow the chaffs off the maze and leave you with solid clean grain. Everyone has that rare behavioral trait in them. Do they come out as being egoistic? Is it their self-image they are always worried about? Are they introverts, extroverts, ambiverts? Do they snap easily? When infuriated, do they have anger surging through their bloodshot eyes? See how they react to different situations, how they handle issues, how they talk, carry themselves around. You have a mass of ideas on how you can identify one's personality, it is up to you to find out how to juxtapose them appropriately then carefully execute them. Your quiver can never run dry on such arrows, never!

Strong Voice Identification

Most of the time, people mistake a loud voice for a strong voice. A strong voice may be soft but comes out as bold and dominant. One can be the loudest yet the weakest in the lot. A strong voice does not necessarily only mean verbal talk, it is about how they verbalize and express themselves. How is this you say? Well, in a strong voice, you can be able to depict one's confidence. This is by how they say their words, how they pronounce them. Are they in haste? Relaxed? What is their body posture like when talking, their facial expressions? Observing such qualities will give you around an answer and soon enough emerge with a finding. With this in mind, subjects will obliviously give themselves away; just get them to talk as you keep that sharp ear and eye.

Action Mirroring

Would you like to be treated how you treat others? Imagine having a doppelganger with all your traits. That is the scenario in this case. Returning a smile or flaunting out that contagious smile and see if they are smiling back. Try some behaviors and see if they will reciprocate or how they react. If they are talking, show engagement, invest as much involvement and interest as they portray and just then will you know whom you are dealing with. However, as some may come out delusive, it will not detract from the fact that it is also a finding and an alarming one for that matter. If you are enthusiastic, try coupling with your incredible investigative intellect and see whether the electricity will flow or repel. It is never really that hard, you will have fun while at it, it is not rocket science!

Identify Deviations

In this context, deviations are the small things that contradict a person's choices or actions. Small inconsistencies pose out as red flags that do not need to be dismissed. When approached in specific different ways, are they conducting themselves in a questionable manner? Are their words matching their actions? What is their diction like? Some of the contradictory actions could be stammering when cornered or when you think they could be lying. Are they scratching their head? This shows uncertainty or indecisiveness. Are they blinking repeatedly? Are they tensed, nervous, calm? It is all arrayed for the eye and ear to be the jury in this court of character and personality.

Importance of Analyzing People

Analyzing people comes in handy because it enables you to know what personality traits you are dealing with and have a head start on have to conduct yourself around them. Known to be a psychological art, people analysis is known for the shrewdness with doctorates in mental health or in the related niche. As you have already seen above, this is an art anyone can practice and come out successful. Some of the importance of it includes:

Easy Relation

Once you know how to communicate with someone, it is all smooth. For instance, take yourself as a foreigner in a country where you know nothing about, not even the language. This will definitely spell doom and prove detrimental for you. You will need to find your way around and get along with people, but only if you familiarize and get to know their way of life. Same case applies here; you cannot get along with people without first having a familiar or common base to start with. You have to know what to portray, what not to portray, when, where, and how and through what means. Not everyone will give the same reaction to your advances or confrontations or even a mere normal friendly "hello". So first, analyze that someone, get to know them better for that wonderful experience, as well as tap into their personalities so that transparency finds firm ground for trust to blossom and thrive.

Perspective Flexibility

Not everyone believes in God, we all have Muslim, Hindu, Christian, and Pagan friends and relatives. We do not relate on religious grounds but correlate on friendly family grounds. This happens when you take time to understand ones' beliefs and principles as compared to yours and respects the fact that they uphold them. Not everyone will agree with you on everything. Boundaries are to be respected and kept and this only comes to notice when you have analyzed someone well enough to know what buttons not to push. Different cultures and societies have their own doctrines and principals or ways of doing things that are often considered as societal morals and cannot be compromised, not even through a simple friendship quest.

Knowing all three sides of the coin keeps you up to par with the do's and don'ts and all the what's not, so that you won't find yourself stepping on one's toe thinking it's part of the stones on the ground as you try to get a glimpse of the horizon. Everyone's tenet is always considered rightful in their own way and in order to relate with them, you have to inquire, listen, compare, and try not to judge. Judging only brings a sense of self-righteousness and this attenuates your chances of getting a genuine ally. Coming out as sagacious rather gives you an upper hand to both satiate your subject on your understanding ability as well as prevent any fuss due to differences.

Understand other's Mental State

In the world we are currently living in, there has been an increased growth in mental illness. Well, not illness that requires medical attention really, but rather understanding and counseling. People require being handled differently depending on their mental state and strengths. Some appear weak, and by weak, I mean are easily manipulated or compromise quite easily due to social pressure or related milestones. It will be much better if you have to know how one thinks, obviously by observing their actions and how they carry their business.

Understanding one's mental state will help you know how to handle them with what degree of attention or engagement. For instance, it is not always easy handling bipolar people for their sudden shift of moods and this may prove to be difficult for someone without the knowledge of such. It may come out as arrogant, unreasonable, or even stubborn, yet it is only a condition that if taken into consideration, could be understood and addressed with special attention and skill.

People's feelings tend to vary and shift as per social expectations or even situations. Getting to understand them keeps you on the right path thus to promote a cohesive relationship as well as friendship. With the right cards played, everyone softens and tends to open up, that is now up to you to look back on how you should analyze someone and find the pointers that will lead you to the possible solutions and handling techniques. This helps one to know what to expect during specific situations and how to neutralize them. It is like having a manual for a toy you just bought— you already know what to do when the controls are spoilt or not functional, how to operate the toy and even repair it if a problem arises.

Understanding someone creates a bond of relationship and a sense of healing to the mental or emotional void they could be suffering from, as well as establish firm common ground that acts as the sole foundation to the friendship or relation. Some take mere things offensively while others shun and easily move on, some are sensitive and others are just pure hard knocks. It is all different with different personalities at play. You will not always be everyone's cup of tea, sometimes even that shot of whiskey!

Speed Reading People

I am sure at some point we have all held a book and perused real quick with our eyes. That is simply speed reading. However, in this context, we are talking about rapid and quick analysis that one does on a person to get to know them. Instead of slowly decoding someone using individual character traits or behavior, you do a collective analysis of what is important and essential. A quick character assessment requires a sharp and attentive mind. You cannot undertake this activity if you have divided attention or easily distracted. It is a race against time or resources and either could vanish without you having completed your goal or achieved your purpose. An act involves the mind, ears, and eyes more as they work hand in hand to hastily process a series of events or occurrences and give effective useful feedback.

You as a self-proclaimed investigator, just like the FBI, critical thinking comes to play here, as you have to update every mental ledger or questionnaire that you have or working on when your subject is under analysis. For this to take play, you must, and I repeat, must be extremely attentive and well conversant with personality traits, characters, and even certain behaviors in relation to circumstances or surrounding.

Speed reading people involve focusing on the important or rather shouting qualities that are portrayed first hand. Not those others are to be easily dismissed, but you are only zeroing in on what possess as a potential lead to a specific trait. Going to the book theory, back in school when looking for a keyword, you would often dash through lines looking for a specific distinguished word that required attention and that is what you are exactly doing here but in terms of people analysis.

You have to formulate a way that you would be quicker processing information than it is discovering or discerning traits. If you lag behind on either, you could lose contact with your subject (that is if it was a meet and leave scenario) or get distracted on something that might shift your concentration from that one person. As you mentally computerize all that data you sieve, cross out the second tier useful traits and focus on the dominant traits that bring much more sense to the activity.

Speed reading a person is something you often do on the streets on a daily basis but unknowingly. Have you ever met that one person that looked suspicious and you thought was going to mug you? What you just did there to determine they could be robbers/thieves is speed reading. You checked their outward appearance, how they walked, and their facial expressions and maybe even how they talked and quickly analyzed to see if your safety could be compromised. There are various methods of conducting a speed reading on someone. It does not have to be complicated or computerize; you just need a functional brain and good senses. Some include:

Scanning

As you perfectly know what a scanner does, that is what you are to do—that simple. Just scan with your eyes as you pick out the important details that you are fishing for. Identifying the key traits or triggering attributes that raise an eyebrow is the main purpose of the eye scanning activity. Just your eyes, nothing much. You are not supposed to set your eyes on anything and everything you come across, but only what is important thus getting a buildup of essential ideas or traits. Your eyes make the first contact with your subject and are the ones that will determine the direction your analysis would take. Focus them at the right place and process some information!

Comprehending

You need a good sense of understanding to easily speed read a person. It all occurs in the mind; you need to be sober and mentally upright. Your processing speed has to be proportionate to the visual speed you possess. Compiling several traits at a go and choosing a dominant one could be quite a task but with the right mindset and attitude as well as skill, comprehending any information coming your way will be a simple task. At the same time, you need to know perfectly what traits fit best at which point and how to cluster them. It is not just about understanding your subject but also understanding different traits and characters. Having a firm and knowledgeable base on them will not only make your work easier but also give you fast results during crucial situations or circumstances that require haste actions.

Concentrating on key points

Eyes can often wander to unnecessary points, either because they seem intriguing or attractive and miss the important bit. It is key to focus on the most outstanding bits rather than just falling for all that meets the eye. For one to come out with factual information they need accuracy and for accuracy to be upheld, then one definitely requires focus, an unmerited focus for that matter. Concentration on the other hand requires discipline and one to be goal or result oriented. If you want a fruitful outcome, you have to invest more of your mental abilities and skills for accurate and sensible results. Ruling out the extraordinary from the norm is what focusing on the key point majors on. The one thing that outdoes the others or outstands. It is like having a rose with thorns but there is that one thorn that happens to be longer and sharper than the others are. Look at it as grain with pebbles among them, remove the pebbles no matter how small or grain as they may appear and remain with clean pure grain.

Best Speed Reading Time

There is no specific time that has been set aside to speed read people. It all occurs when one gets the urge or need to do a quick analysis of someone. Some appear as random opportunities, whereas some can be arranged. Again, it is about speed and availability of chance and resources. Speed reading however indeed has a timing factor to it. That is on first come fast analyze basis. It may be an unheard principle but that is the only known blueprint for success in this field. Once you get an opportunity to analyze someone do not procrastinate, you might not get the same chance again plus you are the one with the need of getting to know your subject more. You will be on the losing end. That split second decision when utilized well could either save your life or spare you many inconveniences. It is up to you to pull that visual trigger and gun down all possible traits for an early assessment.

Speed reading requires a perfect blend of comprehension and unmatched speed. It may not print much of a mental picture in terms of long term remembrance but at the current moment will sure get the job done. It is all about seizing the opportunity when it provides itself, no later moments or fixed times. Again the best time to do some speedy analysis is when someone is not aware, this is because they can compromise their so-called characters and get you played or deceived and fall for the wrong traits. I mean, it happens; we have people out there who are manipulative and good at it. So focus on the identifiable norms when available and in play.

Improving Speed Reading People

If this is a skill that you would like to have mastery in, there are some few things you have to uphold. You need to be keen on when and how to speed read your subject. Not every time you see someone it becomes investigative time. Your chances of fruition in this quest are determined by your devotion and consistency levels, as well as even follow up habits because this is not just a onetime thing. It requires constant monitory activities and updates. Some of the things you are required to do are:

Avoid Distractions

While it Is easy to get distracted, it is also quite easy not to be. Try your best and shun interruptions, as they tend to draw you further from the proper course. It disorients every idea and mental trail of traits you have arrayed leaving them in a mess and prompting you to start afresh. Multitasking also causes a mix up of ideas as you are trying to balance the odds of two different things. Focus on only what is important—your subject and only that. The rest may come after you are through or done with your analysis. Distractions tether you to irrelevant grounds that do not hold much of meaning to what you are doing. Use the logic of ironing some clothes and watching television at the same time. At some point, you will either end up burning your garment or lose a lot of valuable time on something that was not a necessity now, the television.

Identify Key Points

As you venture into the arts, you will notice specific points of interest. Not everything perceived as a pointer is indeed an essential point. Look for few but relevant traits that draw a strong line towards a specific personality or character. You can always compile them and do some further research and emphasis later just for clarity, but speed reading requires quick and accurate results at the snap of fingers. Have some key personality traits on your fingertips, be quite vast and conversant with them and just then you will know what is of more importance that requires direct attention.

Practice

As they always say, practice makes perfect. Well, it is as the words point out. You cannot just wake up one morning and end up a maestro in the field. You have to constantly practice and undergo hurdles, a few setbacks here and there, some failures just to keep you up in good shape and alert. Again, Rome was not built in one day. It takes practice and devotion to gain a proper grip of this skill. You will often at times get confused at the first stages as you try to juggle between quick processing and identification, but in due course, it becomes easy and manageable.

Importance of Speed Reading People

Save time

Instead of having to sit down with an individual and interact to decode their personality type, speed reading comes in handy. A quick analysis saves you both the time and energy that could have been wasted in talking or trying to decipher one's traits. Speed reading points out possible crucial traits that cannot be easily identified when under normal slow interactive analysis sessions. That quick reaction or action portrayed by your subject could prove to be the missing link to your conspiracy or the missing piece of your puzzle. The earlier found, discovered, and addressed, the better.

Enhance memory and comprehension

A small trait that might seem unnoticeable but stuck on your visual ledger can be useful for future reference. This activity enhances your memory in that the more you engage yourself in it, the more you get good at it. It sharpens your mind in terms of both remembrance purposes as well as information processing and analysis. Your levels of understanding as well increase, as you tend to be more open-minded and vastly knowledgeable with the right terminologies and traits involved. As mentioned earlier, practicing this brings out the sixth sense to play that involves all your senses to work in unison for the greater crucial good. Such activities leave no room for faults or errors so an enhanced memory serves just the right purpose to enable accurate understanding and sound judgment.

Sharpens your knowledge on personalities

You will notice that the more you engage yourself, the more you get to know different characters. Well that is obvious, but what is outstanding about it, is it becomes tailored into you to easily identify traits no matter how concealed they may appear. There is nothing more fulfilling like having to crack a code that appeared impossible to decrypt and coming out successful. It with time becomes a part of your daily life and even tends to be a habit. Personalities can be complex and sophisticated to understand at first glance, but in due course with the right informative intake on the relevant fields, you will boast a seat at the high table.

PART ONE

Chapter 2: Para verbal and Nonverbal Language

What is Para Verbal Communication

You could be asking what Para verbal language is. Well, it's all a part of your daily communications modes, it is only that you are never aware of them since they are already a part of you and tailored into your system. Para verbal language is referred to how someone says or brings out words through speech or utterances. It more like depicts the moods one has, that is, is it a happy mood? Are they sad? Grieving? Worried? Anxious? Name it. It all brings out clues and signals that show one's true emotions and feelings. Almost everyone has a mood behind every word that comes out of their mouths. Everything that depicts the true intent of someone is meant to pass a message or communicate something that is always behind it savored by a specific emotion. You will most often notice that someone is calm, in a hurry, shouting, whispering, or even commanding. Well, all those bring out internal support and show one's emotional state.

The way people use their tones and words has always been important because it is the only way they could get their message across and effectively. Miscalculations of hidden emotions or manipulated feelings will always get the wrong messages out or information that is distorted. It is important to know what tones are specified for what kind of moods so as not to misunderstand. When someone is furious or angry, their tone tends to be more rapid and fast with a high pitch. When someone is not in the mood or rather could be bored, their talk or their pitch is usually one with slow and a monotonous delivery.

Most of the time para verbal signals are confused, misread, or wrongly interpreted. With the passing day and daily developments and innovations in society, communication has been crippled in one way or another. That is in religious settings, societal basis, or even cultural terms. The use of tones has been carelessly used whereas you could find tones depicting different moods used at the wrong place or times. For instance, someone who ends their sentence with an upward note could be trying to ask a question or make an inquiry. When they use the same tone in an informative sentence that is passing a message, it could leave one confused on whether it is a rhetoric question or just a misuse of pitch. You can never use a downward tone in an interrogative statement, it will make one mistake your intentions and not take you with the degree of seriousness you could be portraying or demanding.

So Para verbal communication requires one to know perfectly what they want to pass across and how to package it, understand vocal cues as well as the various modes of communications and their effectiveness. Para verbal is somehow related to nonverbal communication since it does not involve words but rather how the actions are accompanied by the words. Paraverbals, once well mastered, you can be sure that correlations and effective communication will take place. Just stick to the right pitch or tone with the right wording and right diction, you will never get misunderstood.

Understanding Para verbal Communication

Generally, Para verbal language can be understood by anyone. You just need the right insight and knowledge on what to expect or look out for. Some of it has us consciously concentrating, whereas some we do subconsciously. Some cues appear less subjected to be controlled by someone since they occur without our knowledge or attention. So the next time you're engaging yourself with someone or in a gathering where there's a lot of conversing, make it a point to keenly look out and put on that investigative hat as you get to understand the Para verbal modes more familiarly. Some of the things that might come out useful or of help in this exercise are:

1. Check and evaluate your effect on people when raising your voice or optic. Try playing around or regulating your voice or vocal levels during different conversations and see how people react to them. This will give you direct and first-hand pointers of what message you have passed through to them by their reaction.

2. Try to have yourself video recorded in a sitting or a conversational activity with others. The more original and natural you are, the better it will be since things will be flowing, genuine, and authentic. As you notice your different expressions and vocal points as you pass specific information with certain degrees of seriousness or message, you will learn more on the Para

verbal modes and how they affect communication.

3. Observing people on a daily basis. This is something that you can carry out on your own at home, school, or even in the community around you. Observing what people are doing in relation to how they talk will stress more sense into how situations or circumstances affect ones' Para verbal modes. Every situation will have a different Para verbal to it. You cannot expect someone who is happy and enthusiastic to be talking in low tones or conversing in a somber mood. You expect vibrancy and an electric touch to their voice. The tone and pitch denote one's mood and feelings. That is if they are sad, happy, grieving, flirty, or even composed.

In learning institutions, there are teachers or lecturers that teach different subjects or course. The way they speak in their classes is not the same way they would talk to you in a one on one basis. Yes, there is the factor of voice in relation to room space or capacity, but also it denotes the moods of subjects and the tone of seriousness to be upheld. It is all a learning curve around nothing out of the ordinary that might push you to enroll for a Para verbal theory course or class.

So just enjoy your surrounding and make it your informative gold mine as you are engaged mentally and physically for accurate and natural responses. Understanding paraverbals is getting the knowledge of people's various ways of communication, analysis, what they mean in different setting and understanding where they are applied and why. Most at times, communication is distorted due to lack of proper understanding and knowledge on the essential small details that are yet crucial.

Nonverbal Language

Nonverbal signals are known to be direct, clear, and precise. They communicate more physically than verbally. Of course, nonverbal communication is conversing without words or vocal involvement. Nonverbal cues communicate more abundance of Intel in a distinct and noticeable manner. They come out as direct and immediate and accompany words where need be to stress on specific points. It could be moods or feelings. Nonverbal communication has been generalized and can be performed by anyone. We at times subconsciously perform nonverbal cues and signals that depict or add on to a message or information. We rarely concentrate on them as we find it a norm or part of our day to day conversations. No one is taught or really tutored on how to communicate nonverbally.

It could either be by our posture, facial expressions, body language, body conformation etc., they all synchronize with the information we are communicating as subordinate supports or helpers. Sometimes people do not feel like talking or opening their mouths so they let their bodies speak, that is a nonverbal conversing technique. Nonverbal cues bring out a distinct nature in our physical voice and talk. They are more genuine as they come out of direct feelings or emotions. This explained further would be that as the mind controls the body, so does the body communicate what is in the mind, and that one cannot be manipulated or diverted. They are a clear and genuine indication of one's mental status and thoughtful nature. Instead of telling someone that you are angry or pissed, you could use your facial expressions to express disgust or even the anger itself. One will just see and notice that there is something wrong. The nature of originality and rawness makes them very effective and accurate when reading and communicating to people. People tend to believe more of what they see visibly rather than what they are told or hear. As they have always said, seeing is believing.

Facial Expressions and Micro Expressions

Facial expressions

Typically, gestures from your face, this means that there are movements of your face that communicate something. It may be a mood or feeling that you are trying to pass across. Facial expressions can comprise from the eyes, mouth, or even facial muscles across the face. The movements of the muscles cause or form notable shapes or rather arrangements that denote something, a signal or message. When frowning, your eyebrows tend to come close together and much lower to the eyes. This without a doubt will not tell you that someone is extremely happy; it could be spelling doom for you. A simple smile, especially an ear to ear one, shows warmth, happiness, accommodation, and even friendliness. All these are paired together to communicate without even you using your vocals. They come out more effective and understandable. For instance, you could be having a soft-spoken person with a soft voice, you would obviously expect them to be loud and deep when talking or ranting but in their case of a soft voice, you could mistake their pitch or tone for a normal simple talk or expression. However, when the same person employs a facial expression showing anger, the message comes across as clear and distinct that the individual is displeased.

Posture

This involves how you conduct your body. Posture has often at times been associated with personalities. That is, it shows how confident one is or how they tend to carry themselves. For instance, someone who happens to have a rather squeezed, small, or contained body conformation or posture most times express a sign of fear or enclosure. They are considered as somehow weak and secluded. However, in the case where someone has an open posture that is in terms of hands, feet, or even shoulders, they are therefore seen as bold, confident, and dominant in a certain way. It all speaks from how you position your body, from the head, is it tilted or straight? The shoulders, that is, are they straight or slightly bent? Outward position or inwards? Your feet, are they closed together or slightly apart, are they crossed? Name it, it is all in how your body is moved and positioned. So just be careful not to send the wrong message.

Distance

How would you communicate to your spouse or best friend when telling them a secret? Will you shout across the room? Will you hold them close, maybe close the gap and tell them in their ear? Well, that is what distance is all about. The closeness of two people as they converse or communicate with each other. It is a communication vector as well related to your body language and as well chained to how you relate to someone. You cannot approach a stranger and close in on them as if you have known each other since kindergarten; they will obviously feel disturbed and uncomfortable.

The distance when hugging or even talking to someone says much about how you feel towards them. This nonverbal cue denotes the degree of trust or relation one has towards you. Well, some might go overboard as some tend to be open-minded and of different personalities viewing life and relations differently. There are those that trust quite easily and those that will take a hefty amount of time to open up and close that distance. So take note of the distance people give you or you yourself give to people and you will note how much it shows your importance to them.

Object

Objects are quite a good tool too. Without even a spoken word or a muscle flinching on your body to communicate, you will have already known something about a specific object. It is all in what the eyes see and process and what knowledge you have on the same subject or object. For instance, when walking on the street, you might meet a police officer in uniform. Without them informing you that they are officers, you will have already known from their uniform and possibly mannerisms.

The objects around us could be every tangible thing that denotes or carries meaning in them. It could be a luxurious car that might tell you of a prestigious and well-financed owner. I mean, it is all that simple objects communicate and keep things in their respective perspectives so as one may not confuse or misinterpret. They could tell you whether you are at the right or wrong place and what you are possibly supposed to be doing. It keeps you aware of your surrounding and how you ought to behave or carry yourself around. They are also modes that send distinct and accurate information that will keep you in line or keep you knowledgeable of a specific person, place, or ideology.

Visional line

This is all about glances. The way we look at things or people communicates much of what we think towards them. For instance, you are interested in courting someone and the feeling was mutual. You will notice that whenever you both meet each other, you steal glances savored with a specific mood or feeling. There is an emotional spectrum represented that one has to be knowledgeable in order not to mistake intent. One could portray disgust, hate, happiness, love, or even domination by how they look at you. Stares provoke specific feelings in people and could mean interest or openness to an invite or friendly talk. Someone staring at you could mean that there is something about you that they are trying to decode and understand. It could be good or bad. However, it is always a form of analyzing someone, scanning them, from their behaviors or characters and understanding them to know how to relate or what findings to come up with.

The eyes as well may come out as a good means of measuring someone's attention in what they are engaged in. You could be talking to someone but their eyes are wandering off, that shows lack of interest or divided attention. The little unnoticeable things people do with their eyes tell a lot about them. Girls are known to roll their eyes more like verbally saying "whatever". All these are on a visional line that is words spoken but through your eyes. Therefore, with this, you should be careful on how you eye things or people for you could be sending the wrong message or info. The eyes being the door to your soul, they help you gather information and process it. That is, it feeds your mind informatively.

Chapter 3: Body Language

Body Language Signals Differences (Eastern to Western Societies)

Body language has proved to be one of the most common modes of communication. Across different cultures and societies, it has carried a lot of meaning and is considered to play a crucial part in relationships. There is always language and speech in the little gestures people make or portray in different scenarios. However, in different settings, it varies in meaning on how people use them or portray them. Most of it comes as obvious since it may come out as common and familiar, but they all carry distinct meaning behind them.

Understanding what body languages mean in diverse and different cultural setting could prove a hefty task especially if you are new to them. It is quite easy to confuse or misinterpret intent for another. Below are some of the vectors use and their differences across different settings.

Eye contact

Eye contact can be conducted anywhere and at any time. Stealing glances from time to time conveys a specific message but in this case, it differs in different settings. In western based countries, direct eye contact may portray assertiveness or even confidence. A bold glance shows you believe and trust in yourself to deliver and a sign of a responsible person as well. In some eastern based countries or even in Africa, some glances beyond the normal brief moments are considered as a sign of aggression or confrontational. Some places it becomes inappropriate or uncomfortable, especially between sexes.

Sitting position

When attending different gatherings or meetings, your sitting positions portray a lot about you in different settings. It could be crossing your legs in some eastern countries, where it's seen as a disrespectful act, or showing the sole of your shoe when sitting, which sends an offensive message (that brings out the notion of why in protests, shoes are often thrown around).

Gender

This is quite common and is experienced in almost every place. What could be acceptable or liable to one gender may not be acceptable for the other. That is for example like shaking one's hand. There are religions that you cannot shake a woman's hand, as it will be considered an offense. The same goes for women covering their head as a sign of purity, whereas in some countries, it shows submission.

Touch

In some countries, different touches show different messages or intent. In most of the Middle East or Eastern countries, they prefer less to no contact as per their cultures. There are very small amounts of handshakes or contact among strangers or people you are not familiar with. In some Arabic countries as well, contact is highly upheld. That is men can even kiss each other and hold hands for long. It is a sign of friendship and trust. In some other western cultures, that could come out as too immoral or even inappropriate. The difference in cultures takes different body language vectors to portray different meanings.

Leg and feet analysis

Legs are an essential part of nonverbal or body language. They communicate a lot about a person without them realizing. It is quite possible to see or know what one is thinking just by looking at their legs or feet. Some leg stunts include opening your legs when standing. This portrays confidence especially when you are well grounded and firm in position. The stance of a wider body makes a person appear bigger thus signaling dominance or power. Another could be when one's feet are close as they stand. This may come out as a major sign of anxiety or could be a sign that someone is feeling cold. When one crossed their feet or legs, it shows a sign of shielding themselves or being protective. To some extents, crossing ones' legs could simply say they want to visit the washrooms.

People tend to walk in different postures or ways. The pace showed by their feet may indicate whether they are tensed, in a hurry, or relaxed and confident. It could also portray laziness or even aches when one drags themselves or walks slowly. One who walks in a stylish manner could bring out a sense of self-consciousness or self-confidence. That is how they walk affects how people see them so they will walk with a specific approach to be perceived in a certain manner. When one cannot see properly or in a dark place, they tend to wander and take zigzag directions or hit obstacles on the way. This show the feet have a sense of direction related to one's sight. Therefore, what one sees, the feet or legs may bring out or complement.

Arm and shoulder signals

You obviously know how to use your arms, well apart from carrying stuff. Arms and shoulders are communication vectors that are used to convey information about oneself. Arms can be used when reaching out to someone whether during a handshake or hug. The ways you conduct the activity will depict the mood or emotion behind it. Are you moving them fast or slow? Moving them more rapidly shows threatening, whereas slowly shows a sign of comfort. Arms as well show moods in that if by forming them to be bigger or smaller. A bigger formation could show happiness or a vibrant spirit whereas a small curvature could show a lack of confidence or retreat.

Arms could be used as tools or weapons. You can use it as a club, i.e. from its shape just clench a fist and you could be hitting someone in seconds. Crossing of one's arms as well portrays a sign of defense, for either protecting yourself or shielding from any incoming attacks. Arms being left open show warmth and a welcoming mood. One's arms can communicate a lot now, it is up to you to know what to employ, how to do, and at which place to avoid confusion.

Eye movements and eye contact

When you meet people or encounter them for the first time, most at times, you steal glances a bit. Well, that could show whether you are going to relate or not. In the same eye contact and eye movements, one gets the chance to analyze and speed read someone. The eyes as they move gather information and tell you about your surroundings. On the other hand, eye movements in itself are a message vector. You can know what someone is thinking or what kind they are by observing their eye movements. They could portray fixed eye movements, which show surety in themselves or confidence or look down or away which might show shyness or lack of interest in something. Through one's eye movements, you can tell if they are lying to you or what intentions they carry.

When people tend to block or cover their eyes, they are simply showing that they did not enjoy or like whatever that is in front of them or what they are seeing. It could indicate they are uncomfortable or simply disturbed. One's pupils also communicate a great deal, that is if someone is aroused or happy, their pupils tend to widen and become big. When they are around negative situations or mood, their pupils constrict.

Eyebrows as we all know as part of our daily facial expressions show moods and emotions. That is whether someone is surprised, sad, happy, or even shocked. Gazing or staring has been known to be an intimate activity. They are also used when showing firm stand or making decisions. That is one can hold their gaze a bit longer when trying to prove a point or emphasis on something serious. Sideways glances, on the other hand, come out as a sign of uncertainty or shyness. In general, the eyes and its movement show and direct one towards their points of interest and will always reflect a bit of what one is thinking.

Handshakes and its importance

Handshakes are widely used and known around the world. They are a sign of greeting, togetherness, or even agreement. Handshakes have different intensity levels to them in relation to the situations they are used in. A handshake might appear strong and firm to show trust and reliability, whereas some might come loose to show dissatisfaction of lack of trust or confidence. In our modern world today, there are varieties of handshakes that carry a different meaning. Some in business settings and even some when relating with friends and family. The intensity of how you squeeze one's hand in different communities speak a lot either about you as an individual or whomever you are greeting or shaking hands with.

Handshakes can determine how people will carry you or conduct themselves around you. A handshake as well could be your only gateway to a successful life or venture; how you conduct it really matters. They give communication life and even portray messages that at times words could not have passed. So as you give handshakes, be aware of what they mean in different settings, whose hand to shake, at what time, and how and in that way, you have the word knowing what you want them to know about yourself.

Facial expressions and Micro Expressions

Facial Expressions

These are quite self-explanatory; one needs no more explanations or illustration. Well it is basically using your face to communicate. Not that you use it as a board and write words on it, rather you express yourself using it. Psychologically, facial expressions have helped a great deal to express emotions and feelings. One's words might compromise but facial expressions can never lie. Looking at it at an angle where you have a dishonest person in play, you expect them to talk a lot and at the same time cover their tracks. They could be good at it, but what they are not aware of, is their body conforms more to what the mind knows and eventually their body's conformation will give them out, which includes facial expressions.

Facial expressions could show a variety of signals pertaining to one's moods, feelings, or emotions. Some of them include:

- Sadness
- Happiness
- Disgust
- Anger
- Uncertainty
- Surprise

Well the list is endless and as you can see, quite interesting that most are not positive clues. It is a combination of muscular activity in different motions or positions that denote one's trait or internal nature. It is something that anyone can carry out and I am sure has used, even the infant babies. Try giving a lemon to your five-month child for tasting and wait for a response. Well of course not verbal, but the face will tell you a lot. How they fold the face, close their eyes, or even move their mouth will tell you that indeed it is bitter. Same analogy applies in people; different circumstances bring out different responses and reactions that can be seen on the face.

Some of the common expressions and where formed comprise of the following:

- **Happiness** – From the eyes brightening up, pupils appear wider or bigger. The mouth tends to widen, i.e. the lips are either spread out or raised and the face becomes more vibrant in nature.
- **Anger** – your eyes and brows form them. The brows tend to lower and become more firm and close together. The eyes might bulge for some and some become small and steady/sharp. For some people, the mouth tends to become smaller or closed tightly.
- **Fear** – One's face shows fear when the eyes widen, eyebrows open up and become raised. The mouth also plays a part, as it tends to open slightly. It is quite easy to know when someone is in fear; their face spells terror and vulnerability.

- **Disgust** – When disgusted, your upper face (eyes and brows) do not move much. It is all in the lower face. I.e. the cheeks, lips, and even nose bridge. The nose bridge gets wrinkled as well as the upper lips become raised raising the cheeks too.

Micro expressions

One does these quick facial expressions in a short time. That is, they are very quick and quite go unnoticed. These specific cues express one's genuine and true emotions. They are the uncontained expressions that one cannot manipulate and rarely control easily.

Micro expressions are very important, as they tend to carry true intentions or feelings of a person. They occur without the person's awareness or knowledge. It is more of a leaked memo from an office that no one in the public was supposed to know about. They often give away the true and genuine trait of someone or their behaviors. There is no single day you can prevent a micro expression from happening or taking place. For emotional intelligence as well as awareness, it is important for one to know these micro expressions to easily analyze or familiarize with people's true selves.

Some of the importance of knowing micro expressions is:

Know deceivers or liars

One cannot hide from such so it is quite obvious that they will give themselves up at some point. Once someone tries to hide their real motive or give out distorted information all to persuade or manipulate you, it will be quite evident from the micro expressions on the faces. It may occur on a specific part of the face but eventually it stands out all from continuous disturbance and appearances. It could occur from a rapid flash or a slightly prolonged action that might seem odd and raise an eyebrow about your subject's genuine intentions. All you need is to be knowledgeable and quite vast with the type of micro expressions in play.

Enhance emotional awareness

Just as drivers on the road use indicators to show the next directions, so does these expressions. They point out possible emotional boundaries or limits that have been compromised or even crossed. They will portray what is really in someone's head or thoughts. Their universal nature of signaling an individual makes it quite easy and understandable for one to depict one's emotional state.

The face housing all emotional traits clearly will give out one or more from time to time when engaged or subjected to a challenge or activity that triggers emotions or feelings. Micro expressions cannot be manipulated or changed by either societal means, religious basis, or even lingual lines. A constant and effective communication cue will always get the point at home.

Liars and How to Identify Them

It is both an easy and difficult task to identify a knave. People tend to lie and get away with, whereas some are just poor in the act. However, we have people who can lie straight to your face with a straight face and you will fall victim to their deception. There are clues and pointers that one could use or notice to identify a liar. All from body conformation to even the words they utter. Liars do not have tags or banner on their foreheads indicating their nature so the following are some of the ways you could identify a liar.

Build rapport

For one to notice dishonest words, you cannot distinguish at only first glance or contact. You need some time to know how the person converses and talks. That tie used will help you gather pointers as to what seems unlikely or does not add up. Almost all of your conversations rather come out as empathetic and tend to work on emotional barriers. Expressing a form of vulnerability makes one open up and feel trustworthy. Taking a slow and gentle approach on conversations will make you approachable as well as give you access to people's real selves rather than coming in an accusatory or cold nature.

Listen more

When you tend to listen more, you will be able to gather a lot of Intel and information on what you want. In the same way, it helps you to gain ideas and conversations helping you find missing links and incomplete stories. When you talk less, you freely give your subject more time to pour out lies and more words which eventually they will entangle themselves in. Knaves tend to speak more than honest people do, as they have to cover up for their lies to sound genuine and true. They tend to hide in the complexities to sound authentic and raw. If you ever have an experience with someone that constantly dishes out words, treat carefully for in those same words lies deception. Just a few of what liars tend to do have been noted and comprise of the following:

- A liar under stressful conditions talkers much faster
- Stress makes liars talk louder (to hide the guilt)
- Senses of anxiety or tension such as clearing of throat or coughing frequently

Observe for behavioral changes

Liars are often not in harmony with their bodies. Its they either will anxious or feel guilty. The same makes them portray physical traits that show. Deception on someone always rings out discomfort of confusion and uncertainty. They chase time or rather do not want to be kept for long in places where they know they have lied in. A liar will always be in a hurry to flee a scene before they are discovered or unraveled. Anxiety and restlessness take over and even at times, fear. Of course, there are those that have mastered the arts and would lie perfectly but for a keen eye, something will not always add up.

Ask for a story backward

Liars tend to have memorized and rehearsed how they will tell you things for them to add up. There is, however, a way to counter their intelligence and that is by asking for an opinion or story from the back. That is if they expected things to start from the beginning and rehearsed from the start's point of view, counter it and bring forth something unpredictable. That way, you have them mincing their words and even mixing up events and in the same way, you will have your liar entangles themselves up in their own words.

Be keen on excessive compliments

Liars are good at sugar coating things. They always have a way with words and that is to persuade or manipulate you. They tell you all nice things just to have you playing along but with this technique, it has always worked. Be careful on the slightest detail that they complement and weigh in to see if it is genuine or just some coated gold chains. Offering praises and undeserving niceties is a sign that they are just playing along to either influence you but in real sense, they show a miss in authenticity and genuineness.

Check for body language

As stated earlier, a liar lacks body conformation. That is they will never synchronize with what they are saying. With the mind already aware of the lying that is taking place, it tends to get repulsive and even uneasy. The fear of being caught or cornered therefore makes one come up with defensive mechanisms to "ease" the anxiety but later on comes out as clues for insincerity. Different parts of the body provide specific signals that indicate whether someone is confident enough with what they are saying or it is just a means of cover up. Guilt in itself is an energy that cannot be covered or sidelined. It has strong pressure points and capability that even the mind finds hard to counter.

Liars provide excessive information

They are a talkative lot. One liar could be backed with multiple subordinate, i.e. to keep it standing and firm. These excessive words are normally dished out to cover up on any loopholes or stories that are not adding up. They tend to talk a lot to sound knowledgeable and factual, whereby all they are doing is clothing up their deception with garments of irrelevant stories. If one thing they said ended up not sounding genuine or making senses, they quickly add up words or issues that indirectly relate to it to either confuse you or drive your attention from the matter at hand.

Liars are repetitive in nature

They always repeat stuff whenever they lack words to say. Phrases that to them felt heavy or substantial are always the go-to to point in their lying. They will repeat them over and over, of course, in different ways just to keep you in a whirlwind or a complex web of confusion. Due to lack of factual information or honest opinions, their creativity levels under stress of delivering tend to shut down and leave them with no option other than to modify, reconstruct, or simply redirect same phrases or lines.

Observe sentence structure or tone

A liar will try their best to show boldness and firmness in their words. This affects how they speak and the kind of words they use. A liar tends to use heavy terminologies or principles that are rather unquestionable or carry a sense of being genuine. Their tone as well comes out as bold but it's a mask put over the fear of discovery underneath. The tone of a liar will be shaky and even savored with guilt. Most of the time, they talk fast to cover up the potholes in their voices. That is hitches or weary voices. Keeping a keen ear to these clues will help you easy decode one's words and what degree of honesty they are on. Well looking from a simple illustration of a child who lies to their parents, their words are usually minced up and confused. They will rarely flow and lack consistency. The same thing even applies to grownups but this time, it is a bit more modified and revised.

PART TWO

Chapter 4: Psychology and Behaviors

What is Psychology?

Widely found to be a discipline only known to the brainy, this has proven to be true yet at the same time false. In schools, it has been a topic of discussions whether to incorporate it into normal studies but some find not liable for it could face exploitation in the wrong ways. Having to study people's behavior gives you an upper hand to manipulate and control them indirectly to your own liking or for selfish gains. On the other hand, some have found it very useful for correlation purposes and for understanding one another.

You may think that you perfectly know what psychology is. Well you might, but most probably, you and the wider public just know the basics. So, what is psychology? What does it entail? Is it for every Tom, Dick, and Harry? Can every mind undertake such a study and come out a professor or a psychologist? Well, psychology has been a career course taken by a few for counseling purposes. Imagine yourself mentally ill with no medication to better your condition or pharmacist to diagnose you, it would be tragic and a highway to distraction and possible self-termination.

Psychology is a branch of science that deals or specializes in people's behaviors and mental activity, how they function and reason out, as well as why some things are done and at what time. It is quite a diverse topic and a goldmine of informative content in terms of personality trait as related to human mind development and social activities. As it is, know that there is always a reaction for every action, so does it apply in this niche. Every action is often triggered by specific attributes or formality configurations in one's mind that portrays their real senses or moral standards and beliefs.

Philosophers delve into psychological studies more to be able to discuss and decrypt a lot of theories and myths, concerning people's thinking and behavioral aspects in different situations pressed by a degree of intensity that would require pure raw outcomes. It is a study that focuses on skills and mental health as well as stability. It is not all about trying to read other people's mind but also to be able to fix what could pose as an ailment not medically, of course, but of mental concern. To know how the mind processes stuff and information is not quite an easy task, but that is why it has been introduced to help counter social ailments that have proven a paralysis agent in people's social lives and even relationships. Every trait is always linked to something, and the body too conforms itself to work hand in hand in sending messages or signals that prove a specific point or provide emphasis on a matter.

Like any other complex field of study, psychology has been a broad phenomenon that requires time, observation, and despicable analytic skills. It requires a specialized form of attention and skill set to distinguish objectively systematic information processing and interpretation. It requires accurate factual and reliable information in terms of theoretical or practical outcomes for distinguishable perspectives. Well, until you zero in on specific human behaviors in different surroundings, most observations or findings are often assumptions judged by sight, heard information, or even performed actions. People's likings, outlooks, and what they process quite vary and you will never get people with a 100% chance of having the same traits. There is always one with that silver lining and one without. Processing the clues dropped or given or that effect and individual requires one of a high standard of understanding and that is where psychologists came from. With their vast knowledge in psychological aspects, they are able to know what affects people in relation to societal and cultural standards or influence.

Psychology itself as a study has been a specialty appreciated in all walks of life and in every social setting with humans (that's obvious, humans talk and relate!). However, it has far spread branches and parts cannot be covered all at once or by a single person. We have different types of psychologists who have made themselves a part of a specific branch and fully tapped into its potential. There is no single day a mere psychological school counselor can handle hospital matters pertaining to the mind's behavior and people's character traits.

However, there is has been myths about psychology and all pertaining to it. It has been said that this is on every simple discipline. Well, to some point, yes and to some, it's a big no. Assuming to be personally experienced in understanding and analyzing people's actions and behaviors does not make you a psychologist. It is more of going into the deeper end and digging much deeper into what meets the common eye or ear. The common eye and ear only grasp what is within the mental grasp. For instance, once you've joined middle school, all on the front covers of textbooks or encyclopedias look all ears and casual but until you open up and peruse the pages, just then will you notice it's not just a 1,2, 3 situation. There are methodologies involved, theories, and analytic procedure involved that require a distinct and special type of attention. Of course, with long overdue practice, one can specialize in a specific field of psychology and come out a maestro with merit and credits to their names.

All that wanted to be mined readers or possess psychic powers or abilities often at times try out psychology with an aim of emerging mental superiors but that is not how things work. It is a process that one has to take. Constant systematically learning and frequent researches as well since it is an accessible discipline that all sandy can access. It requires keen indulgence and focus not to mix up or confuse ideologies. Practice overtime and intellectual investment on courses or informative material will get you going and on the right path. Therefore, it is all about time sacrifice for some mind-blowing knowledge!

Another myth well known is that psychology is common sense. Just as related to the earlier one, it seems easy to just look at someone and come about one or two findings about them. It is not all common sense. This requires a skillset. Looking at rehabilitation psychologists working in hospitals and looking at normal community advisor, you will notice a big difference though all under the same umbrella, they wear different batches to their names. Not just anyone could come about someone suffering or recovering from chronic illness and rehabilitate them. It requires specialized treatment and handling. You cannot handle an eight-year-old child the way you handle a thirty-five-year-old adult. Special stages require specialized attention and touch. So with psychology having branches and all cover the crucial aspect of life from personal mental health to socio-behavioral domains, some of them include:

Clinical Psychology

As the name states, it is primarily in the health sector. Specialists in this field are licensed to help and provide care as well as service to patients in health facilities. It involves interpretation of personality and cognitive analysis and tests. It incorporates both administrations of mental illness diagnosis, treatments, referrals, and even the carrying out of physiotherapy. It is a practice that one can get in most of any health facilities but their specialties are needed mostly in mental health facilities. In such places, one's mental status and wellbeing can be analyzed and tested and a possible solution is given where need be in case of an ailment or an irregularity. Apart from formal subject testing, clinical psychologies involve interviews (one on one basis, or collective interacting) and close observation of behaviors and character traits.

For one to boast mastery in this study, they need to properly understand and know in what way conditions come about, what triggers their existence to life and its manifestation all across a wide range of population in the society. Clinical psychology is in a way similar or related to counseling psychology whereas it is all fixated on mental health and direct subject engagement and analysis. This discipline focuses on special and specific disorders overtime by extensive research in either repulsive behaviors or even compulsive disorders. Therefore, for one to consider themselves a clinical psychologist, they have to be willing to go through leaps and bounds by endless consultations and prescription privileges by going overboard on their educational boundaries.

Educational psychology

Education, as we all know, is an intellectual investment for enlightenment and betterment of thinking and mental capacity. You do not really have to be a genius to know that education is knowledge acquired and stored in the brain. It does not really matter whether it is the environmental changes around one's educational lines or biological constraints that determine if knowledge will be upheld and conveyed but someone's mental abilities. Educational psychology specializes in these fields to determine how they are of relation to people and how it affects them. In short, it decodes the science on how people gain and learn new things (knowledge). Mostly, it affects those still schooling, mostly the youth and those in academic facilities. It is a discipline that might be confused for School Psychology but the major difference is that this one focuses on the general aspect of learning habits, whereas the latter on individual students or learners. School psychology concentrates more on the behaviors of learners as per their learning patterns and issues affecting them directly or indirectly. Educational psychology being the umbrella of psychological study in terms of academic focuses on all types of learners from children to adults. It involves research and extensive analysis which in most times terms its specialists as consultants or low key educators.

Educational psychologies cover the bigger ground on creating institutional balance and diagnose possible threats and loopholes that could affect the education cycle of a given place. The relevant specialist gathers vital information on given institutions or places then point out threats, missing links, and possible diagnosis or rather recommendations all for efficiency and better performance. For one to delve in this field, you must be willing to do research on institutions and companies and come up with effective inquiry methodologies and ways to have accurate and reliable information. It all circles education, it is that simple but also requires a good academic background for one to come out qualified.

Community Psychology

Well, this is self-explanatory. It is all about what happens around your society, in terms of cultural beliefs and community issues. It involves addressing the day to day challenges that one faces or undergoes due to different circumstances. There is no single passing day that you will not face a mental issue, by this I mean coming across something that either reminds you of an occurrence or alters your moods in one way or the other. In a community setting, you are most likely to meet someone with vast knowledge or experience in handling societal issues. They are mostly disguised as community psychologists. The ones you run to when in a relationship scuffle or misunderstanding. When your child or youth needs counseling and rehabilitation assistance, these are the people behind it. They at times choose to specialize in specific aspects of the community or people. You may find some who deal with the elderly, some children, and even parents. They have the whole community covered.

Acknowledging that the everyday society undergoes its own fair share of challenges, mental health has always been a key factor to uphold. With a mentally ill society, there will be no development, proper cohesion or relation among its members so community psychology is a study undertaken for the greater good of keeping the society mentally healthy and upright. Of course, they do not pose as doctors but their resources and abilities allow them to evaluate the communities' amenities, how they affect the general public and possible ways of improving them. Community psychology involves community research in evolving times in relation to changed behaviors, character, or traits or even the way of life of people.

Child Psychology

In the 21st century, there has been an alarming rate of depression among the youth and mostly children. Every day, there is a broken family somewhere with a child or youth caught in between the rubbles of the falling castle. Often times, children tend to seclude themselves with the notion that no one understands or really cares about them. Well, any parent has at some point counseled their children on a matter or even an occurrence that wrecked or scared them mentally. Child psychology involves helping the youngsters cope and get over life's misfortunes from either death, divorce, loss through either rejection or even transitions from schools or residence. It addresses children suffering from issues related to their development, i.e. disabilities in school, academic paralysis, or even mental illness caused by circumstances or developed over time as health issues.

There are very many ways to identify if someone is suffering from a mental ailment, especially if it is a child. They will get less active or extremely active (in some cases when trying to overshadow their problems), some will get withdrawn from the society, get introverted (yes, it is a personality trait but some comes about because of pressing issues all in the head), or just suffer from adjustment disorders. The main job of a specialist in this field is to identify the problem (because most will not open up on what is ailing them), bring forth accurate results, and present a possible diagnose to the issue. It involves a one on one engagement with children and trying to help them open up as well as share a couple or two of what makes their chests heavy laden.

A parent or anyone in the society, who has the authoritative mindset and is knowledgeable of the constraints under review, can be a child psychologist (well, I mean it is all about talking to them and providing solutions right?). This requires a specialty in the relevant discipline as you know different problems or issues require a different approach of which a mere parent or advisor could be lacking. You need to have specialties on how a child's brain works and what triggers which traits or reaction and under what circumstances. It is all in the mind and addressing mental health requires a skillful and specialized solution, one that counters the primary problem and provides an effective long-term effect of health and recovery.

Spiritual Psychology

This is an area of psychology that requires a lot of knowledge and specialty in terms of spiritual matters. Many mysteries engulf this specific section. Like how do supreme beings operate and under which jurisdiction? This requires one's devotion and an open mind because quite a lot of times, different faiths do not necessarily agree with the doctrines presented in other religions thus threatening the comprehension process and cohesion of them as a whole. Of course, diversities matter and understanding them takes a lot of time and even mind power. That is where spiritual psychologists come in. These are people who work on faith related boundaries and topics to bring out understanding and terminological information that people find hard to understand.

Spiritual psychology involves carrying out psychotherapy in organizations or institutions. For such a controversial topic, not anyone can handle or tame the wave of this rocky sea once in debate among people. Everyone feels accustoms to their own beliefs and nothing can sway them. Spiritual psychology also involves connecting spiritual matters with one's wellbeing and how a higher power influences oneself. Religious leaders could be termed as the typical spiritual psychologists to some point but this covers a wider topic than just spiritual matters and connections to different faiths.

Social Psychology

This just as it states involves the social lives of people and their day to day interactions with one another as well as their surroundings. It surrounds the wider topic of perceptions, beliefs, and even social influence. This focuses majorly on the "whys" and "how's" of people's lives and characters. Like for instance, why did someone act or react after some time of an action being done to them, why not immediately, maybe even why do strangers on a pathway tend to stare at each other then quickly look down or aside when walking. It is all about behaviors in relation to people's characters and surroundings. A study pushes on to create experiments or live examinations to see immediate reactions and results pertaining to why something has been done and the triggers behind them.

This branch of psychology is not health-related and therefore does not include treating people or health-related services. It is not about treatment or assessment of mentally ailing individuals but rather on the possibility of helping people social margins like how to raise an adolescent, why children suffer from marital violence, and suchlike topics that affect the society directly and indirectly. The word social bringing out the surrounding aspect refers to a person's habitat as well as areas surrounding them and how it affects their behaviors, adaptability levels, or factors needed and even acquired during such processes. It is a trail of human responses and methodologies involved to reach certain pedestals of an individual's social developments.

Rehabilitation Psychology

This is now common to everyone. Rehabilitation, which is essentially correctional services offered by councilors, is one of the widely known in almost every place. It involves helping out those suffering from chronic illnesses and recovering from it. Some of the ailments are normally acquired or even passed down generations. The specialists in this field provide assessments and analytic services as well as psychotherapy to the affected subjects. The type of assessments conducted is neurotically or emotionally handling issues related to disabilities. Rehabilitation psychologists work hand in hand with neuropsychological specialists in collaboration with health practitioners as well as medical professional.

This is a discipline that majors with the disabled civilian community in one way or another due to ailment has extended effects or newly developed conditions. From brain problems to behavioral issues connected to the mind, a rehabilitation psychologist works on diagnosis and consultation pointing out possible causes and solutions to each problem. From children, youth, parents, to the elderly, all have a spot at the specialist's table for service and inquiries regarding their mental health as well as other chronic illnesses or disabilities they could be undergoing. With proper evaluation and analysis, they carry out family therapeutic services, individual comprehensive treatments, as well as give prescriptions as per the respective ailments. Therefore, this being a special branch of psychology that leans more on the medical domain, one has to be medically well informed and educated well enough and licensed.

Developmental Psychology

It majors on the developmental aspect of people with their surroundings. That is, how people end up bonding with each other, how bonds are created and established. Primarily how emotional ties come about and what is really behind their existence and blossoming. Development psychology focuses on comprehending how traits triggered by emotions and feelings manifest themselves to the outside world, possibly how to manipulate or control or contain them. It does not focus on diagnosing or treating mental conditions but rather their development and growth or synchronization process in one's system in relation to their surroundings. How behaviors are nurtured and watered by different activities to become what they are supposed to be or reach full potential. Just like how a farmer plants a seedling, overtime watch it flower from a bud until it sprouts and blossoms in the sun are what development psychologists do. Observe, analyze, compile information and come out with a theological result that is factual and time tested.

Sport Psychology

This is a sport related discipline that involves athletes and sports people. As much as an athlete may be out there conquering the arenas and stadiums, they have their own problems they are facing. A sports psychologist helps and goes on a mental journey with the relevant subject for them to be at their peak best. It is more of handling off filed situations that affect them in the track or field. In case of injuries or backsets, the specialists through therapy sessions rehabilitate them. It, in turn, helps them cope with transitions, changes, or even perceptional problems that may affect them. Sports psychology is both a service branch of psychology as well as a research-based niche. One practicing this discipline has to do both the groundwork (research, data, and information collection) as well as the rehabilitation bit of advisory services. Their work incorporates finding out how an athlete's involvement in a sport or organization may affect them or their performance in one way or another, i.e. the relation of physical injuries to one's mental health or stability. Misfortunes inflicted on a subject and what consequences are to be expected as well as the possible remedies. Of course, with sports, a person's success is the only goal and the specialists being considered as part of the end goal considering the presence of hurdles that could pose as threatening as well uphold this. Therefore, a sports psychologist handles both health and emotionally related issues pertaining to the sports domain, just in case you developed a profound interest in the arts.

Importance of Psychology

Building of relationships

The common basis of friendships or relationships is through interactions. There is no common base of understanding where people do not understand each other. For one to be effective in conveying a message or communication, they are supposed to be accurate and factual in whatever they are portraying. A proper relationship is built on trust and trust is firmly set up on a foundation of transparency. For one to be termed as transparent, they have to be like an open book, that which one can go through and be able to gain or understand a few things from. Take an example of a new family that just moved into your neighborhood, you be not expected to openly invite them to your residence and show them around as if you have cohabited for centuries. You are expected to take baby steps in first getting to know them and what kind of beliefs they uphold. It does not necessarily mean that if you have a slight difference with someone that you are not supposed to relate, you can have an understanding as well as a difference. In every place you are, there are its own societal or cultural beliefs that tether them towards specific or certain behaviors. That is now up to you to know more about them and how to go about them, both for your convenience as well as your peace of mind.

Once you have a common ground with someone, it shows trust which has resulted from your interest of wanting or getting to know how and why they do things the way they do and what triggers them. For one to get along with another, you have to know and note vulnerable points or boundaries that they possess so that as you interrelate, you will know what grounds to trade on and not to. It is all about getting to know more about someone's behaviors, traits, or even personality to know how to handle them or conduct yourself around them. Building a relationship is like building an engine, every part must properly synchronize with the other leaving no loose end or overly tightened sides for efficiency and convenience.

Improving Communication

This is an obvious significance as to why psychology is important. Psychology helps you know what to say, where, around whom, and how to say it. For instances, it would be very inappropriate for a biology teacher to get into a physics class and start on with a lesson. Of course, there will be a lot of miscommunicating in terms of terminologies as well as confusion and a lot of unnecessary talk. More like describing flower's inner parts to a mechanic does not hold much relevance really. With the possible barriers of smooth communication addressed and properly handled, one can be able to pass down a signal and expect a message back in context with whatever is under review.

Communication is a process that must be followed to the latter, though it does not seem like something that could cause an uproar. Truth of the matter is poor communication or miscommunications could alter a signal and send the wrong information. All this caused by lack of proper measures set aside to properly analyze data or convey a specific message. It is better to know what one means or is trying to say when they portray certain traits or behaviors. Another simple illustration is a dog. When it is happy, it will wag its tail. That study has been done and proven. Same case to humans, there are always reactions or traits that give out your inner motive or intention and reflect rather on what you feel inside or emotionally conveying and the only way they can be understood and accepted is if they are communicated properly.

As a child grows, they learn word by word, from what they hear from the surrounding and mirror it in the attempt of communicating and expressing themselves. They pick signals from people as well as give their own when displeased or in distress. That is communication psychologically linked with behaviors. Therefore, an overall summary would be that for one to communicate, they have to have a full understanding of what they are portraying first. Secondly, they need to understand if the recipient of the message is comfortable with handling whatever data is coming their way. Putting all into consideration a neutral ground is always and will forever be essential in improving one's communication. That can vary from common engage, common emotional or mental abilities, i.e. are they able to process whatever's coming their way, is it understandable, is the feedback going to be as expected?

How the brain works depends on what it has challenged to work on or undertake, and the only way to know its full capacity is communicating to it or airing possible solutions of doing and how it reacts or behaves will have you know what communicative lines you stand as per the feedback. Of course, it is not an overnight sensation; it requires practice, devotion, openness to new ideas and ideologies to improve to a higher mental ability or improved way of thinking that will both be fit for effective communication.

Building Self-Confidence

Self-confidence as the name originally suggests involves the first subject, the self. You have to first start up with yourself and ensure that mentally you can handle anything that comes your way that is within your abilities. Self-confidence comes about as a means of trusting yourself in any situation that you will be able to handle and finesse your way around. Once you are mentally decided and able, it is now said that you can tackle any handles that involve your reaction around people as well as theirs around you. Self-confidence is enhanced when you trust your senses and you firmly know what you can handle and to what extent. Believing in yourself to undergo any challenge posed your way is one way of portraying self-confidence.

Gathering the courage to open up starts with simple inquiries like in an instance, you would not expect a newcomer in a school to make immediately friends. They would first take their time to know what kind of people they are surrounded by, just then they can open up and explore each other. The trusting process as slow as it may be is the only way to build that confidence because you will want to be accurate with whatever it is you are handling. That way you will know what buttons to push and which ones to avoid. So build that confidence, get to know someone, gather your facts right, then execute them one relating them to your findings to stay in line. As a builder lays bricks on a house in a systematic manner, carefully yet skillfully to avoid errors that could cause a threat to the inhabitants, so does psychology matter in once confidence build in gradual time to understanding of behaviors and mental abilities.

Know people's behaviors

Getting to know someone's behaviors gets one to understand how they operate and tend to think. You can never behave the same with someone even if it is an identical twin. There is always one trait that will set you apart from the lot. Knowing one's behaviors is getting to synchronize your ways with their thinking or rather trying to fit the shoes and see things from their perspective. Once you get to understand one's views or character traits or reactions, it will be easy to relate with them and establish a relationship. Take it in a scenario where you have just bought this new machine that you know not how to operate. You will definitely check out the manual for guidance and pointers for the do's and don'ts. That same analogy applies to people. Knowing one's characteristics will keep you in like on where to tread on and where not to, what to communicate to get a specific reaction. There is always something that triggers reactions and emotions. Knowing them will help you correlate with people much easier and effectively acknowledging boundaries or limits.

Knowing one's behaviors is not all about relating to them. At times, getting to know people helps you as an individual know whom to avoid or keep off for what they possess. Some people carry around vibrations that end up either being toxic or affecting an individual. It is as if knowing which rather waters harbors crocodiles, which forests harbor snakes, and so forth. It is good to know the effect of people's presence in your life and how they influence your decisions or traits. Some may tend to lead to the right directions, some to build and inspire, whereas some are pure leeches, sucking the life out of you. So know that person. Get to understand their way of thinking and doing things before engaging yourself with them. It will save you a lot of time as well as peace of mind.

Origin of Behaviors

Well a behavior is not something like a chemistry or physic subject that was discovered out of the blues. These things have developed within people in their different stages of life. Behaviors come to be inborn as well as acquired. Behaviors are traits that can be contagious or rather transferable from one person to another. What most people do not know is that behaviors just like personalities can be developed and nurtured over time. It is like a tree that one has to water, prune, treat with pesticides or insecticides, and take well care of if you desire fruitful results or outcomes.

Looking at this from a psychological approach, behaviors are manuals that are encrypted in someone's mind that make them react or behave in certain ways in relations to their surrounding or circumstance. It is a lifelong learning theory that one will never complete studying or gaining information from. Behaviors come about because of interaction with people and the environment at large. Let us take for an instance, an infant baby. This small human has been born with zero mileage in their brains functionality. That is, they are all new and like an empty book awaiting information to be written. As they grow, they tend to act as per what they have been raised with. Their adaptability levels are normally nurtured or influenced by their parents. In terms of mannerism, it is a parent's duty to keep them in line as they impart disciplinary actions to bring forth decent behaviors and mannerisms, more of garbage in garbage out. They mirror actions and traits. For a child to come out with strong traits or behaviors, their perspective of things often makes them relate differently to other people.

As we will come to understand, new behaviors are learned through new operant conditions. One's outlook or doctrinal principles also bring forth different behaviors across the board. The ways people are taught in different settings on mannerisms or behavioral aspects affect how they think and more like manipulate them into acting or reacting in certain ways. It may sound like a complex phenomenon, but it is simply a mixture of measurable events analyzed, experienced situations (directly or indirectly), and observable happenings. It is all in the look and hear aspect of life. You see a snake, you quickly look for an object to hit it or run away. That is already a mannerism or tendency that is already in someone's brain that snakes are dangerous and can kill you. So using the same analogy, behaviors develop over time through either experience or observations from the society.

Apart from exterior forces or influence, behaviors also develop from an internalized aspect. That is internal events such as emotions or feelings. Thinking can also be considered as part of it. Feeling or emotions as we all know are triggered by external events or happenings around us. The constant or gradual occurrence of these things tends to affect and influence one's behaviors. That is, the more a specific event happens, it will push or make someone act or behave in a specific manner. Let us look at the small infant baby again. A small baby from birth cannot talk, for a fact. Their only mode of communicating is through crying. When a child is distressed or requires attention, at all times will end up crying and cry some more (it is always nerve-wracking yet beautiful in every way). It is their behavior since they are used to it getting them quick response and attention. It will be the case until the child learns how to talk. Behaviors will either be of a repulsive nature to counter or neutralize a situation to their liking or just their mode of survival in situations.

How Behaviors Develop

We all know over time that behaviors are developed or acquired, but how do they end up being part of a person? Behaviors are variegated in actions and are quite vast in nature. They come about as a result of integrated approaches and challenges into different phenomena in their surroundings. That is, they are influenced by what goes on around them. Their way of adapting, coping, or even overcoming the same situations is what we call behaviors. It being a survival tool, it changes in different settings that cannot connect with or support.

Behaviors often are affected by differences in people traits or even societal pressure. People are born into behaviors, whereas some are influenced into them.

Being born into a family of vegans at first will force you into taking vegetables since it is what is always at the table. As you grow, it will be a norm and in the same way do behaviors develop through gradual manipulation or continuous practice. Most factors that affect one's behavior or development of it are academic aspirations (i.e. goals, ambitions, dreams, futuristic educational intentions), parents (upbringing, mannerisms imparted into oneself, disciplinary measures, or even copied or behaviors rubbing off from the adults), all to societal expectations or constraints.

Factors that affect one's behaviors are:

- **Age** – of course, age is a common and obvious factor. One's age will determine how they behave around people or in specific situations. You can never expect grown-up adults to be playing with mud or crying when denied something. Behaviors vary with different stages in life. As one gets older, more mature traits kick in and make one behave in an "adult-like" nature. It is all about changes in brain chemistries as it goes and develops acquiring new Intel or informative content to make them adapt or conform well. Age being a key factor gives one time to undergo stages or trial and error and learning through results of what they do. That is reactions to new or already set mannerism and their relation to them.

- **Environment** – it is often said that someone's behaviors and traits often reflect their upbringing and where they have been brought up. One's environment affects their behavior in that they will practice what they see, hear, or find being done or conducted around them. Things openly done tend to rub off as a standard level way of living or as the norm. There are situations as well that force individuals or leaves one with no choice other than behaving in specific ways. Some are good, some are bad. The social pressures and doctrines pout into people or follow rub off on individuals. So environmental influence is all about manipulation and synchronization already to set standards or constraints.

Chapter 5: Personalities

Simply put, personalities are individual differences in terms of behavioral traits or characteristics. It focuses on how people tend to carry themselves around, think, talk, or even relate to one another. Personalities distinguish people from the other in terms of what they mentally possess and the theories likely behind their characteristic patterns.

Personality Traits

Personalities vary from person to person. There are many known to human nature but only a few come about as common or dominant. They include:

Openness - this is a trait just as its states reveals a sense of transparency and fewer boundaries involved in every aspect. Someone who is known to be open is said to be free with life and knows no closed doors or barriers. They are firmly enterprising people, ambitious, and even adventurers. For someone who is adventurous is known always to want to get to know or see something new. That is, always open to new ideas. They are often curious and willing to go through that extra mile to know something extra or eyebrow raising.

They possess a functional and effective sense of imagination since they are often creating possibilities and different approaches in handling issues. They come out as appreciative in terms of art and their surrounding or anything that came about because of brainpower. This is always a trait that you will find in someone who has considered warm and welcoming. They are the type ready to embrace new life and ideas in all forms and sizes. An open book is always easy to read and write in. Some come with such like traits, easy to get along with and even understand. Strongly they have fewer sophistications and complexities in their ways of doing things. New experiences come out as intriguing to them and something out of the ordinary would definitely be a tickle to their fancies.

Conscientious – This trait is commonly known as a "serious" one. It is found in highly organized individuals who prefer working or moving about according to their priority lines. Little are they swayed, easily distracted, or even carried away by passing glances. They always feel obliged to get things done even if it means getting out of their way as long as the job is done, they are satisfied. Possessing a strong sense or feel of responsibility is their number one mark as they always come about as obliged to stand out and take over.

They are low-key leaders with strong ethics that drive them into achieving their goals or plans over time. Someone with conscientious traits is known to be dependable. That is, you can always count on them to get things done. Putting your confidence in them gives you peace of mind that things will be done or happen. They never fall short or rarely fail (everyone is prone to failure, no one's perfect). They have high discipline and are self-contained. Not much or reserved really but have themselves together character wise and how they conduct themselves. Possibly holding themselves in high regards? Well, could be. They are good planners, often at times are the ones left with organizing things, and never fail in their tasks. They are the "go to" people whenever you require a sane, serious, or even bold opinion concerning matters or issue. More like the big brothers.

Extraversion – from the word extravert, this is a straight commonly merged with openness. This comes out strongly among people who are outgoing, always out mingling, socializing, and again open to new adventures or quests. An extravert is a bubbly talkative person who always has a way with people through associating those conversing with them quite easily and getting along. In every clique, there is always that one person who is the life of the party. Constantly electric and spreading that positive vibes that end up being contagious. Extraversion most at times is inborn, well some acquire it, but it requires patience and trust on one's side. Extraversion includes easy trusting and transparency. Assertiveness upheld these characters come out as cheerful and bubbly. Easy to get along with as well as relate. They never make things hard for others. They have the social connecting factor always bringing people together. They come out as light-hearted, easy goers, acceptable, and easily adaptable in the community.

Agreeableness – not necessarily a yes man but easy to reason with and converse with. It is a trait common merged again with openness and extraversion to some bit. One who is agreeable possesses kindness and a collective yet calm composure. They have a helping heart that is always willing to go beyond its limits or measures for the other subject's wellbeing. More like sacrificing for happiness or to ensure the other is in peace. They tend to be more of sympathizers and are compassionate. Rudeness and harsh talk have never been their portion. For a fact, they avoid such situations by playing the neutral card or the advisory person. They easily trust a person and open up easily too. They believe in transparency as the only means of correlation. People with such traits are quite vulnerable to manipulation as they are not judgmental or strong-willed as much. With their calm and peaceful nature, agreeable people possess a rosy personality that yet is rare and even after a backlash or hurtful situation; they heal quickly and withhold no grudges. They are easy forgiving, trusting, loving, likable, sociable as well as dependable for their sense of loyalty.

Neurotic – this is a trait found in people who are mostly skeptic. They rarely believe in luck rather they question it. They tend to worry at about everything that happens or is to happen considering the odds not being known. The anxious type that will always overthink, overanalyze, redo and undo things whenever they do not feel satisfied. This trait often grows in someone and could come out and cause depression if not contained. It is like a ticking time bomb of a hand grenade that only has a safety pin between distraction and peace. Emotionally unstable people are said to be neurotic because they are constantly thinking on the negatives rather than the positives. Things like, "what will happen if I don't..." "What will I do if..." there is always a shadow of worry and mistrust in situations or people that surround them. At times, it reaches a point where one might end up secluding themselves hoping things go well. It somehow relates to an introversion kind of topic but indirectly. Introversion involves being reserved and unsociable not worrying and anxious. A neurotic questions the "how's" and "what if's" looking at flipsides instead of a direct path. To some extent, it comes out as a strong and useful trait as it gives someone both sides of a story or rather the two sides of a coin meaning that whatever the outcome of a situation, it was already expected and prepared for, instead of surprise occurrences or under-analyzed or thought of things.

Personality Types and Traits

The Composer

This is rather a composed lot as the name suggests. They appear to be somehow introverted but the thing is they take time to warm up. They are quiet, shy, and at times appear to be difficult connecting to them. They are like a gift box that has been wrapped with a simple paper but inside is gold and all niceties imaginable. They come out as spontaneous and very approachable once they get a familiar ground with someone they trust or uphold. They are always up for plans and turning up is never an issue for them as long as it is people they are familiar with. They come out as open-minded and extremely fun to hang around and be with. They believe in the notion of you only live once and therefore utilize every opportunity they get to enjoy life embracing their present life. They believe in adding value to both themselves and others and so it is quite normal to find them imparting more wisdom into themselves as they are in quests of making more friends and meeting new faces. They are not the typical introverts who find pleasure in secluding themselves or locking themselves. These personality types enjoy exploring new grounds and getting to experiment on a lot of this, spearheading issues and possessing as trendsetters. They are inventors and love looking into new ideologies and principles that would add more value into them.

The composer often appears with the following traits:

Introvert – they are quiet and mostly observing more than they talk or speak. They do not socialize that much as they feel it drains or detracts energy from them. They are like solar panels that after use or extensive engagement in something, they take the back seat to recharge or regain momentum once more.

They are more on internal thinkers than outspoken people are.

Sensing - they are a bit sensitive with their surroundings and aware of what happens or affects them that is entangled in their lives. They appear as detailed oriented and more into the specifics of an issue rather than the general outlook. Are quite observant and more into how things are done and work observing to gain full detail. They always appear realistic and live on the current here and present life. Not much of futuristic people, but those that take life one step at a time

Feeling – in every decision they make or engage in, they put their emotional values steadfast. They are the type to follow their hearts than just doing what the mind or surrounding says. That makes them strong-willed and independent in terms of decision making. They are tactful that most of the times is empathetic and always plays the peacemaking role to avoid all sorts of scuffles, arguments, or conflicts

Perceiving – of course, with someone open to almost anything, they are perceived as flexible and adaptable to their surroundings, that is flowing with the wave and tend to get carried away forgetting of their current timelines. Not rule abound, are always up for new tasks.

The Visionary

These are one if not the rarest personality type that is around. This is because as much as they are extraverted, they tend to prefer big talk about this on futuristic lines and basis. They loathe small talks or anything that does not challenge their thinking or reasoning. Not in many society situations will they thrive since they do not quite often find a match or someone of like mind. Mental stimulation is what drives and prepare them in their day to day lives which is something that most people do not like, thinking too much or too hard. They come out dominantly as intelligent as well as vastly knowledgeable of key issues that affect the society or a crucial in one way or another. More like geniuses. They are as well detail oriented but this time in terms of theoretic topics and factual basis. Stating the obvious and the complexities involved as well as the dynamic that could affect or influence an issue. Their approach to information is one that is logical and objective, especially where it could line on an argumentative side. They never want to be considered wrong since they have done their homework right and have just about the right information to quench a vocal factual fire. They are never afraid or reluctant to question issues that do not satisfy their mental states. If a thought is not justifying enough, it is rather dismissed unless it has some logic or reason behind it.

Traits of a visionary:

Extravert – they are always around people feeding their mind with knowledge. With their energy, they are able to engage in argumentative topics and take initiatives. Since they are considered brainy and quite perceptive, they tend to talk a lot more than listening. Always outdoors, they use their enthusiasm to involve themselves in the surrounding or happenings.

Intuitive – they possess analytic skills that few possess. That is they can acquire a great deal of information and come out with credible facts in complex issues or ideologies that are hard or challenging to understand. They have a high sense of imagination, this helps them see things on a three sixty degree perspective unraveling every detail that can make sense and compile them into something factual and knowledgeable. With high creativity, they can never be swayed; in fact, they trust their instincts more and rely on their minds.

Thinking – this is quite obvious since they are brainy. They follow logical grounds rather than their hearts; that is they do not follow their emotions. They come out with raw truths and prefer calling a spade a spade even if it means hurting or overlooking one's emotions or feelings. They would rather tell a fact than sugar coat something that will not make any sense. Protecting feeling is ever in their vocabulary, not even if it involves them. To them, the head is of more importance than the heart.

Perceiving – they always keep their options open for new info to trickle in. That is every source that proves useful will have them open and flexible. They move with the wave where need be and quite adaptable when it comes to things beyond their power or reach. They have a fun side to them too; they can be playful and not mindful of timelines. They do not believe in rules or things that bound their ability to soar to greater heights.

The Nurturer

This is a lot that prefers to take their time to grow with something, take a step by step journey to make sure something has reached its full potential. They are termed as philanthropists—always generous enough and giving back has never been an issue to them. In other words, selfless. They think more of others than themselves. Once they believe in something, they will uphold it and believe in its ability or influence with a lot of enthusiasm. It is a kind-hearted group of people that is warm and welcoming to new options or people without criticism. Other people's emotions and feelings appear to affect their mode of function, as they are sensitive to such lines. They believe in cooperation, cohesion, and correlation to get harmony in all they do. They also believe in giving their all and investing in all that adds up to a greater good or bigger course through awareness and coordination. They act as supplements or catalysts rather they bring out the full potential in someone, all the best in them.

Traits of a nurturer:

Introverted – their open nature is rather selective. They are quiet and reserved. They take time to process issues affecting them and others to come with effective solutions or ideas. A strong trait is that they are self-sufficient and can work pretty much well on their own. A nurturer is someone with the entire winning cards on their sides and so what they are doing is dishing them where need be. They appear comfortable being secluded or on their own. As much as they give out, they also run out of ideas and need time to rejuvenate themselves or recharge. They internalize their thinking processes and are known to be quite thinkers.

Sensing – upholding other people's emotions means that they possess a sense of sensitivity. They believe and trust in factual material that comes out as knowledgeable; that is they are sate with the specifics. Present realities often times affect their logic thinking, as they tend to work more on the realistic or pragmatic lines. Their lives rotate or revolve around the present and less of the future. They are aware of their surrounding and synchronize with it. They have a feel of what is happening around them and prefer first-hand experiences. Their antennas are always high and functional to capture information or grasp whatever it is that interests or influences them.

Feeling – they work well on emotions lines; that is considering others and how they feel and behave towards different situations. They tend to follow their heart more than their minds or logic. They are empathetic and tactful in all that they involve themselves in. For one with a selfless trait, it is expected to sacrifice a lot even if it means detracting from theirs to build others. With an emotional touch to them, they come out reasonable and understanding. The type of person that would listen to you and put themselves in your shoes to try understanding you more.

Judging – for a strong personality, one is often strategic in all they do, say, and cannot have room for faults. Nurturing is more like mentoring so perfection is upheld. They are disciplined and well organized in all they undertake. They have to keep the right facts with distinguishable margins and sense into them. This breed upholds strong and firm work ethics that keep their eyes at the price as well as tethers them around their subject's interests and needs. They like following a routine based program that keeps them in check with their schedules or routines. They also prefer checklists rather than random flying ideas. They possess futuristic traits, that is, they focus on the future and what is to come or expected and plan for it beforehand.

The Thinker

These are the brains, with a capital "B". They are the engines of many institutions and corporates. Most brilliant ideologies and theories come up as results of their brainpower. Comparing to other personality types, they are arguably the smartest and the ones with most sense when it comes to logistics. Their main line of work is complexities as well as overwhelming materials. Easy is basic to them and basic is boring so you already know what tickles their fancies. They never find pleasure in anything that seems mere or accessible to all. They are more of the elite thinkers. Those that close down the curtains in those debate contests or intellectual competitions. Discrepancies are their profound love and patterns that are entangled against each other; that is things that require the use of "brain power", what you would typically say as overthinking that eventually makes you tire.

With a sharp people reading ability, trying to lie or take them in circles would not be the best advisable thing. They create situations, situations do not create them. Their creative thinking and innovative nature do not give them time or space to delve on practical things but rather on other issues that tap into their abilities.

There are unbound in every way imaginable. They are the types that if you locked them inside a concrete room with no doors, they would still find a way out. Strange huh? These are geniuses and inventions are their weaknesses. Their solutions are often at times if not all unbiased, insightful and accurate with a distinct nature and touch to it. In their godly nature, no problem ever lacks a solution no matter how difficult or twisted it may be appearing.

Traits of a thinker:

Introvert – they require their own time to think and come up with stuff. Specialized concentration requires some solitude and deep thinking. They are self-sufficient and depend on themselves on almost everything. They are the "still waters that run deep", conserved and all but once they take the center stage, you'll be at the back seat for a long time. They seclude themselves to recharge and refresh their intellectual quivers for more creative and brainy material. They find comfort trading alone as they believe that at such times is when their mind is working overtime to come up with masterpieces and state of the art ideologies.

Intuitive – they are inborn creative with an out of this world imagination. They come up with things that are unheard of or rather rare and priceless. Complexities are their norm and find them more interesting than normal things that do not challenge the brain. They are also introspective. With their mindsets, they are more future-oriented since as creative, it is always about developing the next big thing. Their instincts are their sole drivers, as they do not rely on hearsay, rumors, or information that seems biased and baseless. Creative minds often hold themselves in high regard since they know their potential, effect, and influence in the society.

Thinking – a thinker primarily thinks and thinks out of the norms. It is not just the mere processing of information but decision making on basis of logical facts and ideas. They follow their heads and not the heart. Logistics come before emotions or feelings. They would rather address an issue sidelining emotional effects that could compromise or manipulate its efficiency or effect. They come out as strongly factual, possess a firm stand, and ground in their opinions. They are natural whiz kids with a spot in the society knowing and unknowingly. Their mental capacity allows them to fit in in any setting since they contain a piece of useful abilities essentially for the greater good.

Perceiving – as earlier stated, they can fit in any setting, as they are easily adaptable. Their flexibility rates make them accessible and approachable. They can easily ride a wave and later on tame or outdo it. They flow with the tides and can synchronize in any situations. Their minds have the ability to psychologically prepare them and equip them with the needful behaviors or traits to fit in. They are spear headers and prefer leading in projects and commencing with them. They rarely keep timelines when things are of importance, which is the urgency to complete and overcome time bounds. They are fun to be around and playful as well. Rules and regulations are often questioned and their relevance in a place. If not applicable or strongly effective, they are broken or bent.

The Commander

This is the general and commander in chief with a sense of entitlement to rule and tower above all. These are leaders with an inborn ability to command respect by their actions and behaviors. They do not go around with pumped chests but their presence itself addresses a special form of authority. They focus on external issues that are handled with logic and rationally. They possess a high sense of intuition as well as reasoning. They look at things from a higher authoritative point of view. Taking charge of situations and circumstances is what fuels their behavior more and gets them going. It is a trait that comes out as a natural like the one they were born for it. From their outward appearance to behavioral aspects, there is something about the commanders that is outstanding and separates them from the lot. They are more of the alpha male of a group, one whose word seems to always final during opinionative situations. Their opinions are often trusted since they come out as dominant and possess a sense of responsibility. Obstacles and milestones are their sole thriving grounds where they find opportunities to take charge and lead forth or command possibilities to fruition. They are self-aware of it and that makes them tread carefully on the kind of decisions or ideas they give out. They are the wavy and unsettled tides that yet run deep.

Traits of a commander:

Extraverts – leaders are always around people so that makes them sociable and easily approachable. With leadership qualities, they are expected to be more energetic and active as compared to the other lot. They constantly are moving from place to place taking charge and conquering. They enjoy and feel obligated to take initiatives as they are always at the forefront of issues or matters. They are always the first to feel the heat of any burning issues as they address it head on. With a lot of enthusiasm that they generally have to possess, they come out as outgoing and adventurous people. They find pleasure in exploring new grounds and challenges since these might make them feel destined to rule. Another strong trait is that they talk more often than you would expect them to be listening. They are constantly giving insight, advice, or even commands on issues and matters surrounding them.

Intuitive – a leader is one with a mindset of overcoming and conquering. That makes them creative with a strong ability to come up with imaginative solutions. They often think out of the box when it comes to crucial situations. In terms of complexities, they possess analytic skills and abilities that help them set out the chaff from the pure grain to have firm and concrete ideas or theories. They are future-oriented individuals as they worry more on the outcomes of issues rather than the current preparations. Leaders are known for making firm rulings and decisions, always follow their instincts and guts in whatever they are feeling right or does not make sense. They are also introspective.

Thinking – leaders are brainy individuals and often at times come out with logical solutions to problems. Their minds work in ways that make them stand out as dominant and reliable. They make sound decisions and even their behavioral traits are bold and distinct. They follow their heads that is factual based information of ideas rather than emotionally based. Their firm stand does not allow them to give in to emotions or feelings. They prefer having to deal with raw facts and situation instead of sugarcoated or pampered circumstances.

Judging – they will question anything that does not seem right or logical. They come out strongly as organized people since they have to have specific doctrinal lines or principles that they uphold. A commander has high discipline levels since they know they are being looked up upon and leaving room for errors will only weaken their personality. They are protocol oriented people with schedules instead of random plans or plats as well as checklists to keep them in line. They are ever ready and prepared for anything coming their way.

The Craftsman

These people are known to be rational or rather very logical. They thrive in mysteries that involve building or developing issues. They come about as spontaneous as well as highly enthusiastic in all they do. They are perceived as hard to decrypt or predict in terms of their behaviors. They are of the type that you would easily say you know like the back of their hands. They change over time and due to their unpredictable nature, they often at times slip out of the social grasp of understanding and familiarity. You can never know their next move or plan or even try to undo their traits to know how they think. They are generously open to new ideas and uphold fairness and a sense of equality. They are more of detail-oriented, that is on how various things work or function. With their logical traits and hands with ability, they prefer handling matters physically in terms of their skillset and come up established or improve already known solutions.

Traits of a craftsman:

Introvert – they are not often secluded from people but rather appear as quiet and more reserved in different settings. They might end up ghosting up on people after their tasks or work is done. They mostly believe that frequently associating with the general public detracts their energy and distorts their thinking patterns. They prefer processing and analyzing their thoughts and ideas internally.

Sensing - they are quite sensitive with their surrounding and always aware of what happens or affects them in terms of development issues or establishment factors or anything that is entangled in their lives. They appear as detailed oriented and more into the specifics or essential bits of an issue rather than the general outlook. They are quite observant and have a profound interest in the manuals like systems of things on how things are done and working by observing to gain full detail. They always appear realistic and live currently on the here and present life. Not much of futuristic people but those that take life one step at a time gaining all that it is to tap from It.

Thinking - this is quite obvious, craftsmen are brainy. They work to bring up new ideas and solutions and fix some of them. They have a repairing nature. Fixing what is not coming out right or logical and bringing perspectives back on line. They uphold their mental abilities rather than what the heart perceives; that is they do not fall victim to their emotions. Craftsmen are creative and often or not come up with new ways of doing things or handling problems. They always have a solution or theory behind each situation. They come out with raw truths and prefer coming out raw yet even if it means hurting or overlooking their feelings.

Perceiving – they have their options open for additional ideas or theories that add more value to them. Every source that proves useful will have them open and flexible. Their flexibility makes them move with different tides where need be and that makes them quite adaptable when it comes to issues beyond their discipline, power, or reach. A craftsman is never a dull person so you can always expect some fun when around them. They possess playful traits and not mindful of pressuring timelines. They do not believe in rules or matters that affect or bind them or their freedom to flourish.

Understanding Peoples Wants

Well, humans appear to be as if books sealed and wrapped in boxes. You will never know what is in them until you open up and explore. There is no single day you see someone's moods or emotions highlighted on their forehead. People tend to react or behave as per their emotions or feelings. Things or occurrences around them affect their mannerism and reactions. Understanding someone takes times, as we all know people are quite good at concealing emotions or internal occurrence. A similar analogy to this would be an ailing person. Looking at them from the outside, they will look definitely normal and well, but the only way to understand or find out their problem is by testing them out. That is the same case in this scenario. Understanding people needs a step by step mode of approach. That is you cannot go straight to asking someone about something that seems to affect them. The best mode would be first to identify red flags. How do you do this you ask? Red flags in this context would mean change of behaviors or mannerisms in a person. Is it how they relate to you that has changed? Is it the habitual traits? Are they sad? Withdrawn? Well, name it; there are many pointers that could lead you to understand a person.

Understanding someone is like getting to read their mind in order to know how to conduct yourself around them or treat them. It takes quite a deal of patience to get to know someone, their wants, needs, likes, and dislikes. For one to relate to you, there has to be a sense of connection or trust, in most cases where it is someone you are relatable to. In the case of a stranger analyzing someone requires a special set of skills, but not that special to be termed as complex. One should be able to know personality types as well as character traits. Proper analysis of behaviors or outcomes of people's mannerism will help you know how to relate with or to them. Understanding one also requires a sense of commitment and readiness to compromise.

There is no single day that you will get to understand someone without putting yourself in their shoes or situations mentally. Get to first analyze the external traits or signals as you close into internal ones (emotions and feelings). Less talk and more listening is a strong point of understanding someone. There are many pointers that one can be able to acquire from how people express themselves. Is it their body language? Is it the type of gestures they are portraying? Is it their voice, their pitch? More attention to such like things could get you to your point of interest.

Understanding people tend to lie more on the "why" aspect of things. Why are they doing a certain action, is it questionable? Why are they talking or doing things like that? The "how" aspect comes in, in terms of now involving yourself in either a neutral perspective or a helping point of view. Understanding someone involves decoding, analyzing, and coming in or intervening in specific situations that need or require your touch to them.

In order to understand what someone wants, there are some guidelines or things one should take into considerations. They are the factors that will outline your level or degree of success in such a quest. However, some of the myths pertaining to the subject include:

Few societal behaviors are seen as explicit

The intentions or motives behind certain actions or behaviors are concealed. Rarely or few times will you find people exposing their true inner sense of emotions to the world. People would rather prefer to die an internal slow and quiet death. That is, most resultant behaviors portrayed or showcased mostly conceal the genuine and true emotions and feeling of a person. Whatever "demons" they are fighting are contained inside them and often hidden by some actions or reactions. However, some of those actions portrayed by such like people would be easily decoded if you took time to analyze, understand, and read them. That is trying to "crack the nut". People say that hiding their true emotions tend to protect them or the people around them, which is something that could be said or done by people of that nature could be hurtful or raw enough to seem alarmingly a concern. So for one to understand an individual, it is best first to keep more focus on empathy rather than just sitting or giving forth time to hear out someone. Not all words or actions carry true intent. Stay woke! The first step would be considered as establishing trust and transparency as well as nurturing some rapport amongst yourselves.

People have little to poor memory

It would be logical to say that people have their own problems and issues that they are processing in their heads. This means that the world does not always revolve around you. The same way as you were born alone and underwent and experienced life's challenges and hurdles as an individual is the same way you won't expect people to be a part of them. Things that especially do not influence or involve them are easily discarded or dismissed. Whatever it is that makes people remember even to the slightest detail of something is when they are either involved or affected in one way or the other. Other than that, expecting them to hold to account all your life occurrences would have you in for a rude shock.

Similarities in terms of situations and happening tend to make people remember you more than their difference. For instance, if you went on a camping trip with several friends and some friends of your friends, the things that make you have common grounds – similarities will often make you remember things that happened or involved you, that there will be a strong vivid explanation or reference point that will keep the event in mind for long. Therefore, it is always about similarities, things that tie you together or make you relate. Is it dressing habits? Talking habits? Another perfect instance going back to the camping analogy would be if you have a friend who does not take alcohol and the fireplace drinks the whole lot, then your sober moments with your ally will come out more of connecting than the ones with the intoxicated lot.

Everyone appears to be emotional

I know it may sound exaggerated but people possess strong feelings and emotions towards different things. That is at specific times, you will notice people with extreme reactions to situations. The traits portrayed or rather the driving force of such reactions is the feeling or emotions invested into the mentality of the person in relation to the situations. At other moments, things come out as heartfelt or personal. It is not wise to think or conclude that everyone is okay since they are not showing signs of turmoil. Seeing someone and assuming they are dry and sandy could only mean that you do not know how to analyze someone properly. No one ever speaks themselves out fully or 100% unless triggered by something that releases the outburst of emotions therefore releasing all that the mind has harbored. People are just reserved, contained, and trying to tame their "demons" alone. They are like grenades. That is, things that anyone can touch and walk around with, but once the safety pin is out, it is all distraction. People have a trigger point. Every kind of personality has that one trait or behavior that comes about because of extreme pressure of challenges, that is the safety pin. So for one to decode such people, or find their way around such, it is wise to be sensitive and gentle in your approach. Once you know the degree of one's sensitivity or emotional boundaries, tread with caution.

The Art of Persuasion and Influence

These two have been a topic of discussions in many forums across the board. Persuasions and influence are key traits that people have used from time to time to their advantage. These come out when in need of something or a following. Question is what do they really mean? What is persuasion and influence?

Influence is the state of social or mental dominance over someone or something. This gives one the power to control or manipulate ideologies and norms around them to work to their favors that is, gaining command and mileage as a sense of power over something. When someone is termed as influential, their word is always found to be final or rather one to be followed. In order for one to gain influence of people or situations, they have to master their environments or circumstances and find missing links or counter links that could bring them leverage and a platform of dominance. Influence is seen and taken as a long term effective act that has a grip on some for a long time.

Influence can be positive or negative; it could spell doom for people as well as spell fortunes for others. Being influenced means that you are under one's control and can only walk by their lead or footsteps.

More like being puppets. You will be swayed and directed on what seems to be another person's ideologies, theories, or principles. Being influenced is being removed or indoctrinated into something that you previously were not aware of or did not believe in. You will be introduced to another person way of viewing things and perspectives that will have an effect over your judgment and known reasoning.

Persuasion, on the other hand, is the art of pleading or rather influence of words in order to change one's reasoning, beliefs, or principles. We have all practiced this in one way or the other at home or even in society. Persuading someone means that you have to make them see things from your point of view and discard theirs. This requires heavy factual and sensible information or ideologies to make one change their mind on something. Persuasion also involves manipulating and using whatever leverages that could pull the subject to your ways or theories. Persuading itself is an extension of pleading. In that, pleading will only require you to express your side of reason or understanding, whereas persuading does that but with a touch of leverage that will make your subject see gain or profit in whatever it is that you present. At times, it seems that one is at the mercies of another.

Persuasion has no exact side but it really appears more from the submissive. It is more likely that someone with power will rarely persuade anyone since they have all they need or require making bold and firm moves. On the other hand, a weak person or one who lacks specific things has to persuade their master or dominant to get whatever they desire. Not that powerful people do not persuade but when they do, they always have something to benefit from. It is a give and take scenario. Persuasion is seen as a short term action whose effects do not withstand a long period. Persuading most times is something done to ask for extensive favors. You remember persuading your parents or guardians to get you that gift or toy, how you pleaded and made promises is what we are talking about here. Getting to express your emotions or feeling to get something done for you or handed to you is the art of persuasion explained in fewer words.

Below are a few techniques of how to influence and persuade someone.

Framing

Well, this could be a new term but it is definitely something you have done at some point in your life. This involves the use and manipulation of feeling or emotions to get things done or decisions made. It is an art where one inflicts fear and bends things or ideologies to the negative to show the side effects of things and possible wrongs that could occur. A good example is an insurance sales agent. This is someone that knows how to balance the odds of one's life's occurrences to his favor. That is, as they see policies and give life assurance, they will constantly mention death as a leverage point for you to make up your mind. They use fear and reassurance but what are looking at here is fear, they will use it to show you how your family will be strained financially and how life will be a living hell after a dependable has passed. They have framed you with your own emotions, made you make a decision based on how you felt. Maybe traumatized, disturbed, confused, worried? Well, that is the same analogy here, playing and using emotions to gain advantage and an upper hand over someone or situations that required that extra pressure or pinch.

Ultimate terms

You could be asking what ultimate terms are, well this are substantial and credible words that are used to show the degree of meaning or stress in an issue. Specific heavy words are shown to bring heavy meaning or the seriousness in a matter. That is, it could be a little bit of exaggeration of situations but to show dire need or consequential actions if not undertaken or addressed. Ultimate terms are mostly used when trying to get influence over something or someone. This helps show genuine or seriousness in things. Most of the time, these kinds of words carry a sense of promise or demands. They tend to ring hope or instill fear. That is to command a firm decision or action. Charismatic words are also used in such activities to bring life and a cohesive sense of togetherness. Ultimate terms come out as bold and contain a lot of meaning or show a balance of odds.

Scarcity principle

If this is a new terminology to you, well it could be understood as a method that shows short supply or less amounts of something. That is, it shows an incoming form of distress or calamity if the shortage cannot be addressed. It manipulates one's mind in that you will have no hope in the little that is left and will start fetching for more or exploring new grounds. It strongly brings out a sense of regret that will befall a person if a situation is not dealt with or resolved. The scarcity principle has often worked in societal settings in terms of politics. People tend to rely more on what they lack in the community to get themselves liable and responsible leaders who will deliver and satisfy their needs. Same thing applies in influencing or persuading people; you will be influenced into thinking of how a great loss a situation might turn out to be if you will not do something or involve yourself. You will often find yourself feeling weaker in such situations since you will be left with no choice other than give in and conform to the demands. Scarcity attracts worry and worry calls for urgencies, reflect and think about that keenly!

Mirroring

Mirroring is primarily doing what the mirror does, copy actions. Mimicking one's actions or traits tend to make them see what they are doing from a different point of view. It is more of serving back the same hot cup of coffee that they served you. This gets one to feel hot, others feel when they are treated or handled in specific ways. It is a form of reflections that will influence one to act in ways that they themselves would like or desire. Mirroring is less of reversed action and more of bouncing back of actions or intent. Many times, it is an influential mode of communication that involves emotion and actions. One can mirror actions to get specific reactions or emotions or mirrors emotions to get actions.

Keep it simple

I know that we have been talking of formulas and theories that will help you get certain traits from someone. It does not always have to sound like a complex test or an FBI kind of activity. The secret that makes all this useful and successful is the level of simplicity used. Heavy terms and methodologies only complicate things and make them harder to understand and undertake. Once you make thing easy to understand and portray, your journey or rather quest will be fruitful. As long as you are factual and straight to the point with what you want, you are sure to get results and accurate ones for that matter. Simplicity is always the best. Complexities as much as they bring out a sense of depth and understanding will not always get the job done. Keeping things simple will make you more understandable and relatable. Of course, it is expected that people will not relate with that they are unfamiliar with. Most people tend to trade in lines of reason and understandability to pick out their odds wisely and freely. One with hard tasks or complex operations before them tends to shun and sideline due to uncertainties of the projected outcomes.

Conclusion

If you are reading this, you have been able to go through the whole book. It is an honor to have you take your time and go through this guide. This shows your devotion and interest in getting familiar with your surroundings and the theories that surround it. The main drive behind this book's existence is to show and bring the light to you the reader, as well as point out and illuminate the way for you in this journey. I hope that it has been of great help as well as become a reference for informative analytic purposes.

Now with the knowledge at hand, you have no excuse but to seize the opportunities life has presented to you, to change and take or continue on that journey to self-development and richness. This is only but a guide that points out various ways and so it does not confine you only to the information it relays. Go all out and do your research, as well as consult and try out different and new ideas. Let this book catapult you to the next pedestal in societal matters as well as personal improvement and skillset.

With discipline and sheer determination, this book is just but one of the many arrows in your quest of riches. With gradual progress, aiming for success using this arrow does not assure you of direct and quick success, but how you use it and strategize on how to execute what you've acquired.

Finally, if you have found this book helpful in any way, please feel free to recommend it to others. Thank you!